P9-BYV-665

This Book Was Donated To
Challenger Elementary School

By _David Simpson_

On _his_ _8th_ Birthday

November 4, 2000

Confidence Counts

By Gary Payton

with Greg Brown

Illustrations by Doug Keith

Taylor Publishing
Dallas, Texas

CHALLENGER

Greg Brown has been involved in sports for thirty years as an athlete and award-winning sportswriter. Brown started his Positively For Kids series after he was unable to find sports books that taught life lessons for his own children. Gary's book is the 14th in the series. Brown regularly speaks at schools and can be reached at greg@PositivelyForKids.com. He lives in Bothell, Washington, with his wife, Stacy, and two children, Lauren and Benji.

Doug Keith has provided illustrations for national magazines such as *Sports Illustrated for Kids*, greeting cards, and books. Keith can be reached at his Internet address: atozdk@aol.com.

All photos courtesy of Gary Payton and family except the following:
Allsport: 24 left; 39 right. AP/Wide World: 24 right; 27 bottom right; 28 top right; 31 right; 32; 34 top left; 34 top right; 35. *Eugene Register Guard*: 23 right. Gary Payton Foundation: 37 bottom left. *Gazette Times*/Paul VanDevelder: 22 right. NBA Photos: 24 middle; 26; 28 top left; 36; 37 top left; 40 right. OSU Sports Information: 21; 22 left. Ron Riefterer: 8; 10; 12 right; 13 top left. *Seattle Times*—Benjamin Benschneider: 3 right, 5 left, 27 top; Alan Berner: 29 right, 33, 39 top left; Mark Harrison: 4 right, 5 right, 31 left; Rod Mar: 25, 27 bottom left, 28 bottom, 29 left, 30, 37 right, 38, 40 left; Tom Reese: 39 bottom left; Barry Wong: 4 left. *Sports Illustrated*: 23 left. Troy Wayrynen: 20.

The GARY PAYTON Foundation

Gary Payton will donate royalties from the sale of this book to the Gary Payton Foundation, which provides opportunities in the areas of education, recreation, and overall wellness to at-risk youth who are deprived of basic options in life.

Copyright © 1999 by Gary Payton and Greg Brown
All rights reserved.
No part of this book may be reproduced in any form or by any means without written permission from the publisher.

Published by Taylor Publishing Company
1550 West Mockingbird Lane
Dallas, Texas 75235
www.taylorpub.com

Designed by David Timmons

Library of Congress Cataloging-in-Publication Data

Payton, Gary, 1968–
        Confidence counts / Gary Payton, Greg Brown.
                p.   cm.
        Summary: Gary Payton describes his childhood in Oakland, California, his college years, his basketball career with the Seattle Supersonics, and his turn as an Olympic champion in 1996, using events from his life to illustrate the importance of self-confidence.
        ISBN 0-87833-228-6 (hardcover)
        1. Payton, Gary, 1968– Juvenile literature. 2. Basketball players—United States Biography Juvenile literature. [1. Payton, Gary, 1968– 2. Basketball players. 3. Afro-American Biography. 4. Self-confidence.] I. Brown, Greg. II. Title
GV884.P39A3 1999
796.323'092—dc21
[B]   99-19795
                                                        CIP

Printed in the United States of America
10 9 8 7 6 5 4 3 2 1

What's up? I'm Gary Payton, guard for the Seattle SuperSonics.

I've played in the National Basketball Association since 1990. And I've traveled the world and learned many things, thanks to basketball.

I've written this book to share with you some true stories about myself that may help you. Not so long ago, I was a young kid trying to find my way, too. I've learned that in sports, and in life, to be successful you need confidence.

So sit down and you'll hear it straight from "G.P." I'm going to talk about how to find confidence, how to keep it, and what to do when your confidence crumbles.

Some call me "The Glove" because I play in-your-face defense. Others call me "The Mouth" because part of my game is talking.

People watching me might not understand that talking is the way I learned to play the game. Where I grew up, people in the stands were all over you. So were players, coaches, and referees. If you didn't answer, you didn't survive on the court. I'm not trying to trash anyone while I play. I just challenge people.

Mostly, however, I challenge myself. I shout out loud for myself. It helps motivate me and my teammates. Guys I play against understand. I'm going to talk at you during the game. But after, I'll kick it with you.

Seems if I can hear my self-motivation out loud, then I can believe it. I think sometimes everyone needs to pump themselves up by yelling out words of encouragement.

I love what Jesse Jackson tells kids at school assemblies. He has them scream: "I am somebody!"

If you believe you are nothing, you'll be nobody.

No matter your history, confidence starts by believing you are someone special—that you have worth. No two people have the same game. We all have unique talents. So stand up and scream: "I am somebody!"

Thanks to a supportive family, I always felt I was going to be somebody.

To understand how my confidence grew, you have to look at how and where I grew up.

San Francisco

Oakland—
Home of
NFL Raiders
NBA Warriors
MLB A's

I'm proud to say I'm from Oakland, California. Across the bay from San Francisco, Oakland is a melting-pot community. It's a city of hardworking people of all colors who take pride in many things, including their sports teams.

Most big cities have two sides—shiny and rough. I've experienced both sides of Oakland.

I'm the baby of the family—the youngest of five Payton children.

My family lived in the West Oakland projects when I was born, July 23, 1968. Poor people living on top of each other caused poverty's frustrations to boil over.

You could hear it just outside the door and windows. Yelling. Street fights. Gunshots. I saw and heard things no child should.

I was too young to understand why my family felt unsafe. My older brothers and sisters had it much tougher than me growing up. By the time I came along, however, things were looking up for my family. I got just about everything I wanted, since I was the baby.

Mom and Dad worked long and hard to find us a better place to live. Mom worked two and sometimes three jobs a day. Dad put in long hours as a cook to save enough money to buy a house.

When I turned 10, we moved into a mansion. At least it seemed like one to me. The one-story, three-bedroom house had a yard, good neighbors, and a safe street in East Oakland.

I first played basketball on the sidewalk. Our family hung a coat hanger from our front tree to create a rim and Payton's court.

Gary would cry when he couldn't make a basket while playing at the tree. His daddy would lift him up over the other kids so he could score. His brothers and sisters would ask, "Why does Gary get everything?" I'd say, "He's not special. He's just the baby of the family."
—Annie Payton, Gary's mother

On 41st Street I made fast friends. We played football and hide-and-seek. And we were always on bikes, riding everywhere and falling down. I grew into a daredevil. We bought plastic walkie-talkies, and I'd jump off roofs pretending to play TV characters of an action drama called "SWAT."

I loved 41st Street.

I got hooked on sports by watching my older brothers and sisters. Greg, the oldest, was an outstanding three-sport athlete. Alfred wrestled. Wynette wasn't into sports, but Sharon played softball aggressively. On the softball field, I'm tellin' you, Sharon would punch out boys. Some of Sharon's feistiness rubbed off on me.

Greg introduced me to basketball. I'd go to his games and hang out on the bench. I'd hand out towels and water, feeling like one of the guys. Sometimes players gave me candy or quarters. Best of all, they answered my endless questions about the game. I soaked it all up and loved every minute.

Greg went on to play at the University of San Francisco and was called "Ice Man." The nickname wasn't true. He was warm to me. He always had time to play sports with me. Chillin' at home, we'd set up a shoe against the wall and shoot tennis balls into the hole from our knees. We didn't have enough money to buy those indoor Nerf basketballs.

Greg boosted my confidence by pretending to be a radio announcer. Every shot became a game-winner, complete with crowd noise.

Older brothers can build up or tear down confidence in younger brothers. Greg's positive attention became my foundation for confidence.

HE STEPS TO THE LINE ... HE SHOOTS ... HE SCORES!

9

We played sports from sunrise to sunset during the summer. Besides the basketball court, we played on the school soccer field. We'd play basketball, then kickball or baseball. We could play baseball, strikeout as we called it, with just two people. We drew a box on a wall for the strike zone. If the pitcher threw it by and it hit inside the box, that was a strike. We made up our own ground rules. Over the fence was a home run. One bounce to the fence was a triple. In case you're wondering, I did play baseball until high school, but quit my junior year to focus on basketball.

My first taste of basketball competition came just around the corner from our house at the Jefferson Elementary playground.

I played with older kids, first with my brothers and then on street teams as I got older.

This right here is where my game was born. Playing guys twice my size on skin-chewing concrete hardened me.

Everyone in my 'hood played street basketball. Whenever we'd choose teams, they'd always say with the first pick, "I got young Payton," even though I was two or three years younger than everyone.

Guys from other streets—42nd, Rosedale, High Street, 38th Avenue, and Brookdale—would come to our court, or we'd go to theirs.

Those were some of the fiercest games I have ever played in. No ticky-tack fouls here—no blood, no foul. If we won on our home court, I'd talk crazy and tell the fellas to "get up off our court and get out of our neighborhood."

As you can imagine, players didn't appreciate such tall words from such a short guy like me. A harmless scuffle sometimes broke out until tempers cooled.

During those years, I played my share of organized basketball, too.

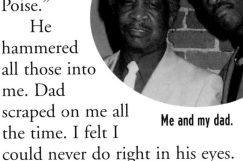

The first team I played for had an appropriate name—We Are Family. Teammates called the head coach "Mr. Mean." I called him Father.

Dad donated his time to coach in the ONB (Oakland Neighborhood Basketball) league. He became a father to many boys who didn't have one at home. Sometimes he bought basketball shoes for those who needed them.

Through basketball, he instilled discipline, pride, and confidence in all his players. He printed T-shirts that read: "Pride and Poise."

He hammered all those into me. Dad scraped on me all the time. I felt I could never do right in his eyes.

Me and my dad.

Until, that is, a game was on the line. Then he'd say, "Let's give it to Gary."

Dad's faith in me during crunch time gave me confidence in myself. I played on his teams for 10 years, and my confidence grew. We went undefeated every year, it seemed, and I averaged about 40 points a game. One game I pumped in 66 points—my all-time high.

My strong desire to play showed when I was 12. Our team made it to the championship game, but I had dislocated my thumb and wore a cast from my elbow to my knuckles. I wanted to play so much that during the first half, I chewed off my cast down to my wrist. I begged Dad to let me play. He wrapped the remaining cast in foam, and I scored 27 points to help us win another title.

Dad (far right) paid most of the cost of our uniforms out of his own pocket, although we did have unusual sponsors sometimes, including Allied Ambulance. I'm the one holding the ball.

Everyone needs a father figure. If you don't have a father at home, seek out honorable men who can counsel you—a coach, teacher, neighbor, or minister. Or call the Big Brothers and Sisters organization in your area.

Jefferson Elementary School is one place I didn't score many points. Everyone there knew me as Gary Payton, the joker.

I didn't like school at all. I wanted to go to school to have fun. I couldn't stand just sitting and listening to the teacher. So I became the class clown. I visited the principal's office all the time. I even got kicked out for throwing my hands at someone's face while saying "Made you blink!" and accidentally flicking their face with my fingers.

I'm not going to lie, my elementary years were a struggle. I'm fortunate my parents and teachers didn't give up on me.

Jefferson Elementary

He always wanted to stay after practice and shoot. He was always striving to be better. That was my first year of coaching the boys team, and they never disrespected me. We won the city championship. . . . That year we had a player named Marty, almost 6-foot-4. Everyone teased him, asking when he'd dunk. Gary stood up for him every time and said, "He'll dunk when he's ready!"
—Janice Doubley, Gary's 7th grade coach

Gary was the team leader . . . . I remember being down 7 to a rival with 50 seconds on the clock. We ran a play to Gary, and he scored. He stole the ball, scored, then got another steal and assist to tie it. We got a turnover, and Gary was fouled. He calmly hit both free throws to send us to the city championship.
—Warren Doubley, Gary's 8th and 9th grade coach

Basketball was it in junior high. We'd get to school early and play in our school clothes and get all sweaty. From the beginning, you could see his confidence. He shouldn't have had that much confidence at that age.
—Marty White, childhood friend and junior high teammate

My Claremont Junior High team. That's me in the front, second from the right.

My years at Claremont Junior High were much different. I loved junior high. I became a B student and met great friends, guys I still hang out with now.

I played basketball and baseball. You might be surprised by my height back then. I was one of the smaller kids in the school at 5-foot-2 as a seventh grader. By ninth grade, I still stood just 5-4.

Being so short wasn't a worry for me. I used my quickness to get to the basket. I figured if I stayed small, I would find a way to be great.

High school coaches took notice of my game, and some asked me to play on their teams.

I chose Skyline High, across town on a hill in an upper-class neighborhood. I petitioned and was allowed to attend, even though I didn't live in the area. Basketball opened the door.

I almost slammed that door of opportunity on myself. I fell into a trap that pulls down some athletes.

I believed things would be handed to me. I figured if they got me here to play basketball, then it didn't matter what I did in class. I didn't listen. I thought I knew it all. I was wrong.

Administrators kicked me off the team for poor grades my sophomore season. I slid downhill for awhile. I cut classes, got into fights, and mouthed off to teachers. If I couldn't play, I might as well cause trouble, or so I thought. In a way, I gave up on myself.

One day, my father burst into my class. I sank in my seat with

nowhere to hide. He marched straight to me with angry eyes and snatched me up out of my seat by my clothes. He pulled me out of class and drove me home. He delivered the worst tongue-lashing I've ever heard.

Once again, the people around me had confidence in me. They had faith in my potential.

If you doubt yourself, stay near those who believe in you.

Gary did have one run-in with the law before he turned 16. I let him wash my car one day. He jumped in and drove around the block. The joyride backfired when he ran into a parked car . . . but the cop let him off because I told him Gary was a good kid. Gary was a character. People see his mean face on the court, but he really does have a good heart. Gary gives back a lot to Oakland and the Boys and Girls Clubs and his family. I'm proud of him as a player and a person.
—Al Payton, Gary's father

It's frightening to think how close I came to throwing my life away with poor choices.

The thought of not playing basketball was terrifying enough. What scared me the most, however, was being home alone.

With my older siblings at school or work and my parents working, most weekdays I'd come home from school to an empty house and be by myself until eleven o'clock at night. My parents would call to check on me, but I was still alone.

I'd lock all the doors. I'd turn on all the lights. I'd turn the TV on and have the telephone close by. My imagination ran wild sometimes if I heard strange noises.

I faced that fear every day by myself. I still hate to be alone. Maybe that's one reason I surround myself with friends and family almost anywhere I go.

Even negative experiences can have positive outcomes when you have a confident outlook on life. Being alone made me independent and stronger emotionally. I learned how to cook and clean and take care of my laundry. Even as a child, my room was the cleanest in the house. Everything had to be in its place. Living on my own in college was no big deal.

Today, friends think I'm a clean freak. When people come over to my house and make a mess, I sometimes clean up right around them.

But I'm getting ahead of my story.

Going into my junior year, Skyline High School changed basketball coaches. The boys program had a sorry losing reputation and finished with just one league victory my sophomore season without me. The girls coach took over the boys program. Coach Fred Noel and his discipline changed my life around.

Coach Noel told me flat out I had talent, but he wasn't going to kiss up to me.

"If you want to play basketball, your grades will have to come up," he said. "Before you can bounce a ball, you'll have to prove to me you are capable of good grades."

With my parents' approval, I went to school at 5 a.m. A few other teammates joined me.

Coach Noel checked us in every morning, and then we hit the study table with a tutor for 3 hours before school. That lasted 6 months. It's amazing how extra studying builds confidence in the classroom.

I proved I could do the job off the court. I enjoyed math the most. I had the most trouble with Spanish. I'd have to get up and recite numbers or vocabulary and couldn't remember anything. That was embarrassing.

My junior and senior years, Skyline teams were kicking—the best in school history, some say. I scored an average of 18.3 points a game my junior year. As a senior, I improved to 20.6.

Doubters turned into believers as we won two league championships and compiled records of 19-7 and 20-5. We had three future professional players in myself, center Greg Foster, and Henry Turner. Eight went on to play Division I college sports.

Our success went to my head. I shaved various symbols into my hair, such as my initials, a dollar sign, or a champagne glass. I wore a diamond earring, which back then was new for guys. The license plate on the 1967 Chevy my dad bought for me read "Mr. Icy." I enjoyed being flashy.

That's because guys on the street left you alone if you were well-known.

They'd say, "He's a baller. Don't mess with him."

My rule was: Either my way or the highway. Gary started doing his own thing his first game of his junior year. I sat him down . . . . He found he could still do his thing within my system. His senior year, I didn't have to call time-outs. Gary knew what I wanted.
—Coach Fred Noel

My basketball reputation made all the top guards in the league want to take me on. Bring it on, I'd say. I thrive on competition. That's what I love about sports: color doesn't matter; family status doesn't matter; money doesn't matter. What matters is performance.

Our team's performance in the postseason disappointed us all. Both years, we lost in the first round of the Northern California playoffs.

The loss my junior year hurt the most. We had the ball and the lead in the final seconds. But I dribbled the ball off my foot and the other team scored to knock us out. That was tough to swallow.

I learned, however, you have to take the good with the bad. Sometimes you're the hero, sometimes the goat. For me, I'll take either one. If the game's on the line, put the ball in my hands. I'm not afraid to lose. Losers, however, are afraid to win. To me, you show your courage by trying.

© 1999 Troy Wayrynen

My biggest disappointment in high school wasn't on the court.

Many college coaches recruited me. It made me proud when college coaches watched my games. I decided on attending St. John's University in New York, for all the wrong reasons—TV fame, big-name players, and a fast city.

But on the deadline day for signing my commitment, the St. John's coach called Coach Noel and withdrew his scholarship offer to me. St. John's wanted a player from New York instead.

The undercut ripped deep into me. They played me against this other guy. I felt used.

What am I going to do? I thought.

That day, I put my fate in my mother's hands. "You decide where I should play," I said.

She picked Oregon State, which was my second choice anyway.

Several days later, the Beavers were a few miles north getting ready to play the California Bears. I drove to their practice and walked in. I sat next to their legendary coach, Ralph Miller, and said, "I want to play for you."

Looking back, going to the small town of Corvallis, Oregon, proved to be the best thing that could have happened. The distractions of New York would have pulled me down. I stayed away from trouble in Oregon and took care of business.

The Pac-10 named me Rookie of the Year my freshman season. The ride had just begun.

I continued to grow in height but not in maturity. My sophomore year, I lost my temper a couple of times during games.

Oregon State's rival is the Oregon Ducks. One night we played at their court, known as "The Pit." The hostile fans were all over me, taunting me and calling me "Hookhead."

I couldn't handle it. My emotions exploded, and I tossed my wad of gum at an Oregon male cheerleader. He didn't duck, and it hit between his eyes. Fortunately, he wasn't hurt.

During another game, I kicked a basketball across the floor after a call I didn't like. I'm not proud of those outbursts. Sports has a way of testing your character. I wasn't passing.

Slowly I matured, thanks to the guidance of those around me.

You need a team around you and their support when you mess up.

He has a strange look—like a frown—and always looks like he's jawing. He'd come to the bench, and people thought we were arguing. He never once argued about anything with me. I couldn't ask for anyone with a better attitude for school, his coach, and teammates.
—Ralph Miller, OSU coach, who retired after Gary's freshman season

From day one, he knew he had to improve. Sometimes he didn't appear to be listening, but he heard everything. You only had to tell him something once. . . . In big games, Gary would say to me, "Coach, take it easy. I'm going to take care of things tonight."
—Jimmy Anderson, who replaced Miller at OSU

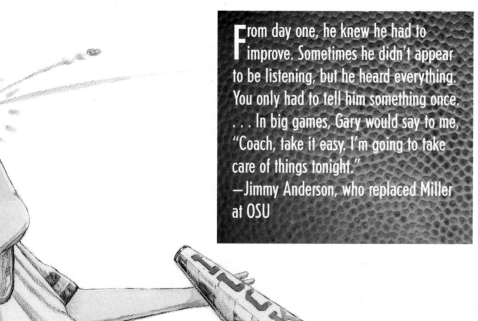

Two sides of the game I focused on at OSU were slipping the ball to teammates and stealing the ball from others. A great assist or steal is more satisfying than scoring, to me.

Assists make people around you play better. Confident people aren't threatened by the talents of others or the credit they receive.

There were games when I was told not to pass so much.

My senior year against USC, we were down by about 20 points at the half. Coach Jimmy Anderson, who replaced Miller, told me to shoot more. I spoke with Dad at the break, and he said

USC Coach George Raveling surprised me with a congratulatory hug after the game.

the same thing. So I did. I shot and shot.

I finished with 58 points (my college career high) and sparked a comeback win. The funny thing about that night was that Mom decided to go to the hotel because we were behind so much at the half, so she missed seeing my magical second half.

Confidence never gives up. No hole is too deep, no deficit too big, when you have time on your side.

Oregon State Highlights
- Leading career scorer in school history with 2,172 points
- 939 career assists ranked second in nation in 1990
- National Player of the Year, *Sports Illustrated*
- Averaged 25.7 points, 8.1 assists senior year
- Started every game in OSU career

Toward the end of my senior year, *Sports Illustrated* wrote a cover story, proclaiming me the College Player of the Year.

I felt on top of the world—or at least on top of the rim for a few terrifying seconds.

I never let those props go to my head. Dad always told me: "You can be on the top of the hill, and everyone will be right with you. But someday you'll be on the bottom, and they might talk badly about you."

I know all this limelight will end someday. So I try not to get too excited or too depressed about anything in sports.

I take it all in stride, remembering it took a team to get me here—family, friends, teammates, and coaches.

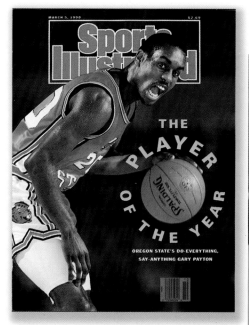

The Payton family: Annie and Al in front, with their children (*left to right*) Wynette, Alfred, Greg, Gary, and Sharon.

The Seattle SuperSonics drafted me with their No. 1 pick in 1990, second overall, and fulfilled my dreams of playing in the NBA.

The first 1½ seasons in the league didn't work out as I'd envisioned.

I'm the type of player that you have to let go out and play basketball. If I mess up, let me make it up down the line with a good defensive play or something.

But I felt if I made one bad mistake, I was coming out. That crushed my confidence.

It got so bad that I wanted to start over with a new team. My heart wasn't in the game.

I didn't work out that much that first offseason. Dad confronted me one day. If I wanted to stay in the league, not to mention be a star in the league, I would have to work harder, he said.

Midway into my second season, the Sonics changed coaches and brought in George Karl.

He gave me the opportunity to play and become a man and a better person in life. He stuck with me and gave me confidence and taught me how to relate to the older players.

That summer, Karl brought in assistant coach Tim Grgurich. "Grg" took me under his wing and showed me how to dedicate myself in the offseason, working out sometimes five hours straight.

He also showed me the importance of working on your weaknesses and always striving to improve. Grgurich is the reason my game went to a higher level.

My jumpshot is what needed the most work.

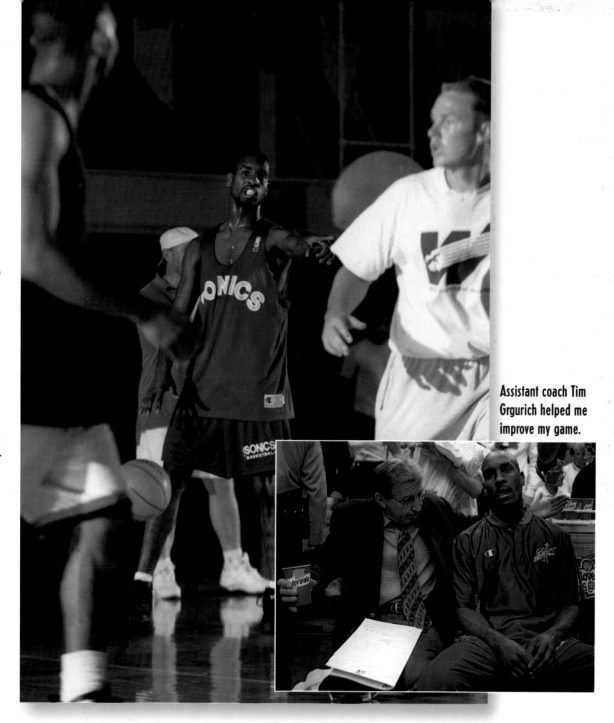

Assistant coach Tim Grgurich helped me improve my game.

Gary's NBA Three-Point Shooting			
YR	FGM	FGA	PCT
90-91	1	13	.077
91-92	3	23	.130
92-93	7	34	.206
93-94	15	54	.278
94-95	70	232	.302
95-96	98	299	.328
96-97	119	380	.313
97-98	134	397	.338
98-99	83	281	.295

More than any other basketball skill, shooting the ball is all about confidence. I've never taken a shot I thought I would miss.

If you think you're going to miss before you shoot, I guarantee you will.

I made only one three-point shot my first season. I made 134 of them seven seasons later. The chart on this page shows how my outside shooting has improved.

There is no big secret how I did it. It takes practice. Repetition of a skill saves it in your muscle memory.

In the offseason, I might shoot about 500 shots a day. During the season, I shoot about 200 times in practice and for about 30 minutes before each game.

Practice, practice, practice produces confidence. Did you catch that? Being good at anything takes effort. Confidence, like a building, is created one brick of success at a time.

What gives me the most pride is playing great defense. Shooting the basketball can be hot or cold, but you can always play tough defense.

Playing defense is all about heart and having the will to move your feet.

During the 1993 Western Finals against Phoenix, I played tight defense on Suns guard Kevin Johnson. My cousins called on the phone and said, "You're holding KJ like a baseball in a glove."

"The Glove" was born.

My confidence led me to prove myself as a defensive player. I made the NBA All-Defense First Team six straight years and in 1996 was named NBA Defensive Player of the Year.

Once you've paid the price of time and commitment, you can go on any court and look confident.

I might not always feel confident, but I would never show that on the court. I always wear my "game face" when I play.

I want to show opponents and teammates that I'm serious about winning.

My motivation does not come from hate or revenge. It comes from my love of the game and my love of competition.

I've found negative motivation might work for a while, but being motivated by love makes you work harder and longer.

Find what you really love to do and work hard at it. That's a formula for success.

There will be times when I don't feel like playing. Maybe my body is run-down or hurting.

Those are the times when my love for the game is tested. The easy thing to do might be to sit out a few games. But when you love something or someone, it's not about how you feel every day or what is the easiest thing to do. It's about your decision to commit yourself and overcome a little pain.

As long as I'm not hurting myself or my team, I want to play as much as possible. In my first six seasons, I missed only two games and had a streak of 354 consecutive games played.

That was threatened many times. One game in Minnesota, I badly sprained my ankle and needed crutches to board the team jet. Someone asked if I'd be ready to play the next night. "I'm good to go," I said.

Teammates laughed, "Yeah, right!"

I did play.

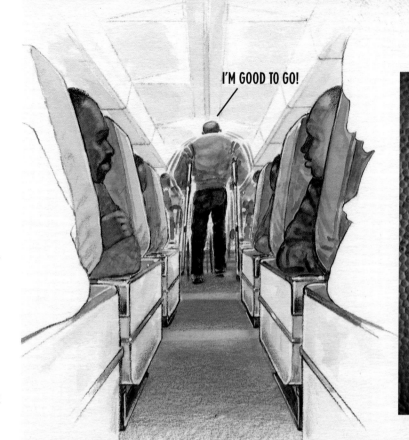

I'M GOOD TO GO!

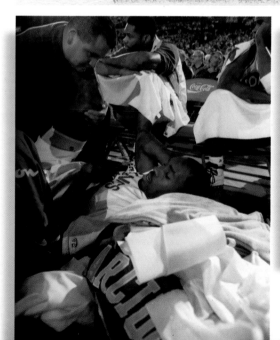

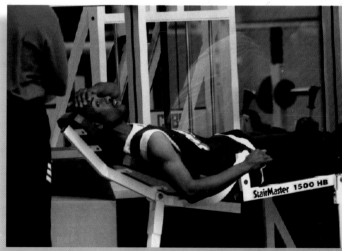

Through the years, I've learned how to condition my body and take care of it. Be smart with your own body—it's the only one you have.

So don't put poisons in it. If you use drugs for confidence, they will become a crutch and hobble you. If you experiment with them, they will blow up in your face. If you use them for fun, you'll become a bad joke.

29

Sooner or later, all players go through slumps when everything goes wrong at once. It happens to teams, too.

After just missing going to the NBA Finals in 1993, we were embarrassed the next two seasons by shocking first-round playoff losses.

Those were tough times. I tried to step up and encourage everyone that we were going to come back—that everything would be okay. Inside, however, I ached. I walked around mad and moody for a long time at home. Thankfully, I could talk about it with family and friends.

Whatever front you put up during life's bumps, you need to let out your frustration by talking about it with people you can trust. Have confidence in friends and family, and confide in them.

The next season, 1996, we were favored to beat Sacramento in the first round, but we fell to 1-1 in the series.

It seemed some fans and the media expected us to lose again. Overcoming history can be difficult. People will say, "Here we go again!"

While past victories can give you confidence, past defeats do not predict the future.

You have to believe you can break free of negative history. I look at each game, each day, as a new chance.

We finally broke our first-round bonds, beating Sacramento, 3-1. We breezed through Houston, 4-0, and met Utah in the Western Conference Finals. The series see-sawed and tension built as we went to a deciding seventh game. Three years before, we were in the same position and lost to the Suns. But we overcame our past and edged the Jazz by four points.

Defeating adversity and history makes victory that much sweeter.

That win put us in the NBA Finals against the mighty Chicago Bulls and Michael Jordan.

Playing in championship games, and winning, is what all athletes dream about.

Our dream in 1996 fell a little short. We dropped the first two games in Chicago and then our first home game to fall behind, 3-0.

When everyone thought we were dead, I'm proud of how we fought back and won the next two games to force the series back to Chicago.

Then Jordan, the best player in the history of the game, took over, and the Bulls claimed another title.

I learned so much playing in the Finals and against Jordan.

Jordan had a fire in his eyes, and he knew when to take over a game in critical situations.

We went into the series just to survive. If we ever get back, we'll know how to win.

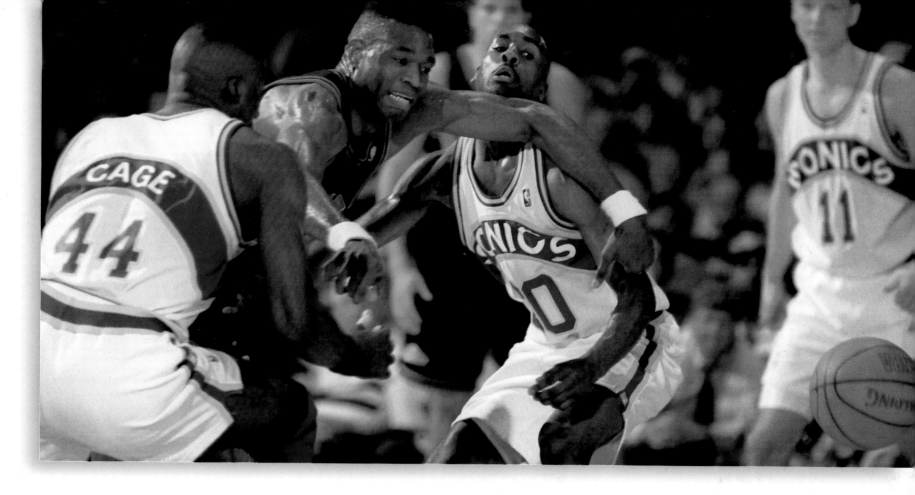

Some might call losing in the Finals a failure. I don't believe in failure. Failure is not in my vocabulary.

If you work hard, do your best, and lose, to me that's not failure.

We were knocked down by a better team. Life's rough, you know. Everyone is knocked down at some point.

Sometimes you floor yourself by making stupid choices. I've made my share of mistakes on and off the court.

The test becomes: Do you have the will to win—to stand up and get back into the game?

33

I didn't have much time to mope around after losing to Chicago. Within 12 days, I was playing again—this time on the U.S. Olympic Team, known as Dream Team III. Being on the Olympic team filled me with humble honor.

Everyone expected us to sweep through the Olympic Games undefeated and win the gold medal. And we did. Winning the gold medal will forever be a highlight of my life.

Another great moment at the Games came when our team met with boxing great Muhammad Ali.

It thrilled me to stand next to him. I followed his career as I grew up and admired him. I have every video ever made of him and have watched them all. Talk about someone with ultimate confidence . . . he predicted victory and backed up his words.

Despite a disease that affects his speech and causes his limbs to shake, Ali showed the world his fighting spirit with his presence at the Games.

My wife, Monique, helped me show off my Olympic gold medal.

Playing on NBA All-Star teams with Jason Kidd is always special for me. Jason, who is 5 years younger, grew up near me. I remember him as a 12-year-old coming around to play street games with us. I'd let him play and gave him pointers. We've been close ever since.

Watching his success gives me a brotherly pride.

The 1995 NBA All-Star game is one that stands out—not because I was the co-MVP of the game. But because my family and friends were all there.

Gary has always been my teacher and always will be. Since I was 15 and growing up in the Bay area, and now that I'm an All-Star in the league, I still listen to everything he has to say. He taught me most of what I know.
—Jason Kidd

B. J. and I connected in our first meeting at Children's Hospital.

I've met many people who inspire me in different ways.

I met B. J. Simpson during the SuperSonics' annual Christmas visit to Children's Hospital in Seattle.

It's never easy going to a hospital, but if I can give someone a boost, I'm happy to do it. In the long run, I think I get more out of it than the kids.

I learned that B. J. was battling cancer and became inspired by the spark and joy in her spirit. We developed a close friendship.

I invited her to a Sonics game in Seattle one night. I dedicated the game to her, made the winning basket, and gave her my jersey.

B. J. fought her illness as courageously as Ali has fought his. I visited her frequently in the hospital, and we talked on the phone.

During a practice a short time later, a message came that B. J. needed to see me.

I got there as soon as possible, but she slipped into a coma before I arrived. I sat on her bed and held her hand. Her family left the room, and I whispered comforting words into her ear. With eyes closed, she responded by squeezing my hand so I knew her ears were open.

Some time passed as I held her.

Then, peacefully, she stopped breathing and her grip relaxed in my hand. B. J. went to a better place.

I felt helpless. No amount of confidence could change her fate. I couldn't save her. B. J.'s death broke me up inside.

Perhaps, in a way, knowing her has saved me. She helps me keep my life in perspective. Her victorious spirit continues to motivate me to help others. Ali once said that helping others is the rent we pay to be on Earth.

I'm proud of Gary that he made it. Not that he made it to the NBA or has made a lot of money, but he had a dream and he fulfilled it. I'm also pleased that he hasn't let his success go to his head . . . . A while back, my friend's mother passed away and the family didn't have enough money to bury her. "How much do you need?" he said. I told him, and he sent the money. He gives back a lot in little secret ways like that.

—Annie Payton

I've tried to keep up on "my rent" over the years by donating my time and money. In 1996, I started the Gary Payton Foundation. Its purpose is to help underprivileged kids in school and to provide safe places for them.

We've raised almost a million dollars, thanks to NBA All-Star charity games, auctions, and basketball camps.

We've contributed to Big Brothers and Big Sisters, helped a private school build a covered playground, donated game gear to schools, and established a college scholarship fund. The Foundation will continue to do great things well after my NBA career ends.

At the beginning of my NBA career is when I started going out with Monique. Turns out we both attended Skyline High, and she played basketball, too. We didn't know each other well because we were in different grades.

I proposed just months after we were together, but our engagement dragged on for five years. I had a stubborn streak in me. For some strange reason, I didn't want to get married until I turned 30.

One day, the Sonics invited me to Key Arena to meet with some

My family is important to me. Like my son, Gary, they're always there to give me support.

kids early before a game. I showed up and found a big box at half-court with a table and chairs. I sat down.

The Sonics' mascot, Squatch, ran out and told me to look at the scoreboard above. Bold letters flashed across: "Will You Marry Me?"

Monique jumped out of the box, with rings in hand. I was speechless. Six months later we married. I was 28.

We have three beautiful children, and I love my family above all else.

Trust is a cornerstone of any relationship. I have two sports agents I trust, Aaron and Eric Goodwin. The Goodwin brothers have been a big part of my life. They are there for me anytime. They are more than business partners. They are close friends.

I spend so much time with teammates, they begin to feel like family. Besides the competition, the next best thing about sports is the relationships you make.

On the court I do have a scowl, but I bust a smile sometimes. I'm not always down to business. I'm into playing pool when I have some extra time on my hands. During the season, I might get out and watch a few local sporting events.

I think it's important to laugh and hang out with friends—as long as it's balanced by taking care of your responsibilities to family, school, and your job.

I know my job as an NBA player won't last forever.

Maybe some day I'll follow in my father's footsteps and open a restaurant. Or maybe I'll do something else.

What matters is that I have confidence that I'm more than a basketball player. I'm willing to try new things.

I have confidence in the future. Do you?

The way things are now doesn't mean they have to stay that way. You have the power to change the score.

So give life your best shot, and remember that confidence does count.

CHALLENGER